The Teacher's Manual
for Three Workbooks

Fourth Grade

Fifth Grade

Sixth to Eighth Grades

Ted Warren

Copyright © 2017 by Ted Warren

Published by The Teenage-Edge & Company

www.teenage-edge.org

ISBN: 978-0-9915847-5-8

All rights reserved. No part of this publication may be reproduced, stored in a retrieval system or transmitted, in any form, or by any means, electronic, mechanical, recorded, photocopied, or otherwise, without the prior written permission of both the copyright owner and the above publisher of this book, except by a reviewer who may quote brief passages in a review.

The scanning, uploading, and distribution of this book via the Internet or via any other means without the permission of the publisher is illegal and punishable by law. Please purchase only authorized electronic editions and do not participate in or encourage electronic piracy of copyrightable materials. Your support of the author's rights is appreciated.

Printed in the United States of America

Contents

Introduction 5

How To Use the Workbooks 6

The Value of Using Grammar To Create Good Learning Processes 10

Teaching Grammar Based on Knowledge of the Human Being 12

Weekly Exercises 17

Fourth Grade Key Concepts by Chapter 18

Fourth Grade Games and Drawings 21

Fourth Grade Workbook List of Grammatical Content 25

Fifth Grade Key Concepts by Chapter 27

Fifth Grade Games, Drawings, and Memory Exercises 35

List Of Content In the Fifth Grade Workbook 37

The Sixth To Eighth Grade Key Concepts by Chapter 43

List of Content in the Sixth to Eighth Grade Workbook 68

Suggestions for the Ninth Grade 71

Sources 73

Introduction

The Teenage Edge

These English Workbooks are designed within the grammar-based learning process that I developed while teaching English in Waldorf Schools for twenty-eight years. With his educational principles, knowledge of the human being, teaching methods, and exercises for teachers, Rudolf Steiner has continually inspired this work. My teacher, Jørgen Smit, inspired me to find new methods of teaching grammar.

The workbooks guide children to use grammar to improve their writing, speaking, and reading. By writing simple sentences and expanding them with related, grammatical elements, the pupil learns directly within the structure of the language. With their solid understanding of grammar, children can develop essential skills: writing style, reading comprehension, building vocabulary, pronunciation, and conversation.

Proper grammar helps children express themselves better. With it, they share what they think, they sense, they love, and how they feel for others. Every sentence in their learning process is important. They learn to be accurate and confident.

Learning grammar also helps them reflect over what they know. They develop more consciousness by placing what they already know from many years of speaking their language into a meaningful relationship. This new consciousness of language builds a healthy self-consciousness, which helps the children eventually discover more and more of the core of their personalities.

By working through examples of writing exercises, rules, drawings, memory exercises, quizzes, tests, and dictations, teachers learn new ways of teaching English grammar. Some children may even use the workbook as a self-learning tool.

In order to make these workbboks available to public and private school teachers the common core standards have been included. The workbooks are a three-part series that include all topics recommended in, *The Common Core Standards, English Language Arts Standards, Grades 4 -12*, published by the National Governors Association Center for Best Practices, Council of Chief State School Officers, Washington D.C. in 2010. You will find some variation in the timing of when subjects are presented in the workbooks.

I want to thank my sister, Anita, for all of her inspiration and support while editing the workbooks and the teacher's manual.

Through the years, all of my pupils have created the mood for learning, written their own examples, asked questions, and challenged our thinking in the classroom. To all of you, I am forever grateful.

Ted Warren

How To Use the Workbooks

The first task for the teacher at the beginning of any school year is to review the level of grammar reached in the previous year. Move swiftly. Cover all of your bases thoroughly. Use a sense of humor. Make it fun and be positive. The goal is to always help them find their next step and thereby build their confidence. They remember and they forget. You allow them to rebuild their concepts.

Teachers need to know how grammar works. Once you have learned how English grammar works, you can focus your attention on the learning process of each individual student. Ask yourself the question, "How do my students learn?"

With this question in mind, you develop meaningful pictures which the children can relate to, preferably from daily life. There are ideas in your pictures, ideas the children may grasp in their feelings as well as their thinking. You use these pictures to present the relevant grammatical idea. For example you introduce the idea of what the noun does in a sentence. Find meaningful pictures of nouns you may present. Present them. Write sentences with them. Then ask the children what these words are doing in the following sentences you give them. Then they discover the answer to your question. When the teacher uses his imagination to teach in pictures, the children`s imagination is also activated in relation to grammar. You awaken new awareness in your pupils. They have used nouns for many years, but now they discover what the noun does in a sentence. This is not an abstraction for the children, but a genuine experience of grammar.

Then you move onto other parts of speech. What do the verbs, prepositions, pronouns, and adverbs do in the sentences? And later you show how phrases and the clauses add clarity, detail, and flavor. You need to guide them into an understanding of how the language works. Otherwise your grammar lessons become automatic and meaningless.

It is important that grammar not be taught as a mere formality. If done in this way, with sentence after sentence being evaluated, while noting sentence parts and types of words in great detail, the opportunity of it being a lasting, well-integrated endeavor is lost. Grammar is reduced to an empty scheme, a routine machine-like process that is rather like a fishing net with no living fish. That is when the children lose interest. Perhaps this is why many schools have dropped grammar lessons?

In a successful grammar lesson, the children are enlivened. As I mentioned, the teacher makes examples of various grammatical functions that are relevant to the children's lives: experiences in the house, in the classroom, on vacation, or in the town. The lessons are planned to involve the children personally. After we have presented the grammatical topic and practiced it in class, we ask them to write their own examples. If every child in the class can make her own examples, rather than repeating the examples from a book or on the board, you know you are on the right path. Bring them to the point where they are asking questions and searching for grammatical relationships between lessons. Then you know you are doing a good job.

How do we make learning grammar fun and educational? How will it become a meaningful activity that improves their use of the language?

Do our methods challenge them to use adverbs more powerfully? Do their verbs become more accurate? Are our teaching methods so good that the children leave the lesson with good feelings in their hearts? You will find the answers to these questions in your own teaching, once you have used these workbooks for a year or two.

Take care of their joy of writing. In the early years you do not need to correct everything. For many children, it is more important for them to write and have fun, than to do everything correctly. Then you may slowly help them learn to correct their own mistakes. Give them good examples of how you would improve their sentences, but do not comment on every mistake. Here you need to find the balance with each child.

Remember that you are continually striving to help the children enrich their experiences with English. Do not get lost in abstractions. If you tell a child that an adverb defines a verb, an adjective, or another verb, all you have done is present an abstraction. This definition should not be a goal in itself. Your goal is to inspire them to use adverbs more powerfully in their writing and speaking.

Rules and examples are given in all three Teenage Edge workbooks. The rules provided are not very important. All they do is provide direction for the learning process. They help in general Do not ask the children to *learn* the rules by heart. The goal is to learn to use the rules so they have them at their fingertips and become accurate with their language. Their confidence will then grow.

Nor should the children remember the examples in the books. Even their own examples should be forgotten. The goal is to continually write new sentences based on their understanding of the language.. The examples they create are building blocks, not finished products. It is more important for them to practice and use the language creatively.

Take your time to allow the children to move independently through the exercises. There is no rush. They need to be confident of what they learn, day by day and week by week during the entire school year. Children need to make an effort to learn. They will become tired so make it worth their while by building their confidence step by step.

When using this workbook it is best to have the children write down all answers in good handwriting. Decide how accurately you want them to spell. The goal is to help children develop their language. You do not need to expect the children to be proficient from the start.

Reading is one of the best ways to learn a language. Ask them to read at home and at school spend time with the children reading their own sentences out loud, in addition to great literature!

The chapters in the workbooks are not written to follow one after the other. They are separate areas of grammar, therefore you can choose when to use which chapter in your class. Feel free to jump from one chapter to another, according to what you feel your students need to work on. Make your own exercises and develop new exercises together with your pupils.

The teacher should know how well the pupil is learning and which challenges the pupil faces. To do this you need to evaluate where they stand in the work and give them constructive feedback. Even then, it is natural for young children to repeat the same mistake until they finally learn.

I also suggest you teach through conversation in the classroom. Then use the workbook as examples, rules, and exercises for them to follow up with at home.

Another method I have success with is to do the exercises verbally in class. I let them answer on the spot and help them if they get stuck. This gives them good practice in thinking out loud while sharing it with others.

Whether they are doing the exercises in writing in class or verbally it is important for the teacher to increase the level of concentration in the classroom in a healthy rythmn. Move from intense moments to more relaxed moments and use a lot of good humor.

Challenging the pupils to work together is always fun. You may use all of the workbooks in the classroom by making pairs or trios of children who work together. The teacher merely sets the rules for their work. Use your imagination to find relevant work for them in pairs. It may be as simple as asking their neighbor how to spell words or to write sentences. Then they can take turns.

Here is a more complicated example of how to engage them in pairs or trios. We can use the parts of speech as the topic.

Partner one writes a simple sentence with three words.

> *She talks carefully.*

Partner two identifies the parts of speech.

Partner two writes a simple sentence with five worlds.

> *My grandmother peels her peas.*

Partner one identifies the parts of speech.

Partner one writes a compound sentence .

> *I eat and I sleep well by the lake.*

Partner two identifiies the parts of speech.

Partner two writes a complex sentence.

> *You walk as fast as you can.*

Partner one identifies the parts of speech.

Partner one writes a compound-complex sentence.

> *I eat breakfast as soon as I can, then I wait for lunch.*

Partner two identifies the parts of speech.

You can continue this type of work with any topic or any exercise in the book.

When using grammar as a tool to improve their learning processes, be brave but careful, as you quide them to improve their attitudes and change their habits. Good attitudes are essential. Bad attitudes may be changed. Good working habits are essential. Bad working habits can be changed over time. As a teacher you hold the thread in the learning process for each child. Each year convince your pupils that making mistakes is normal. They then work to learn from their mistakes.

The workbooks are still valuable in the ninth grade when you review these grammar concepts in their entirety once more. Use the book as a reference. Ask them questions and let them look up the answers in the book using the index or create new exercises at the ninth grade level: ask the class to write a noun, then a verb, an adverb, then an article, then a prepositional phrase and build a good sentence. Find new variations, add phrases and clauses to the challenges you make.

Finally, you may want to use the workbooks yourself to learn English grammar and then create all of your own examples with your students..

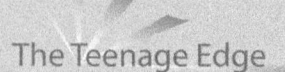

The Value of Using Grammar To Create Good Learning Processes

What is the true function of learning grammar? By learning and practicing grammar, the learning process helps the child develop its thinking capacity. Learning awakens the child's consciousness. In the lesson, we guide the child into raising her consciousness based on something she already knows within the language. She raises something she is familiar with, to a new level. The language is the means. It provides an objective element for her learning process.

Learning and practicing grammar enables children to reflect over grammatical patterns so that the words and sentences of the English language no longer stream randomly in their memory. Children discover how the language works and learn to use it effectively. Their language receives a backbone.

Before the introduction of grammar, children learn their language through imitating the sounds and rhythms of speech. With their feelings, children grasp the words and recognize pronunciation. What changes with the formal study of grammar is that the quality of different words and how they correspond is introduced consciously; the tension between one word and another is sharpened.

Grammar helps children prepare for TOEFL tests, Pre SATs and the SATs. In one's life it is important to speak and write while using grammar properly. Professional employers will hire people who know how to use their language well. There is a certain kind of respect that ensues when a person expresses himself with correct grammar. One is understood more clearly.

One of our main educational goals is to guide children to create their own concepts about whatever they encounter in life. The concepts children create build confidence in their learning processes and add maturity to their personality. This is a major challenge for every teacher. How can we guide children through this process? First, we need to discover how each pupil learns. Then, we can identify where our pupils stand in their learning process in each subject. When they work with grammar, we will discover whether or not they have found a meaningful relationship between its many parts. That is when we know they are developing their own concepts in grammar.

Rudolf Steiner suggested that teachers start by guiding their pupils to experience conclusions. Then we help them make judgments about those conclusions. Afterwards we guide our pupils into placing their conclusions and judgments into a meaningful relationship, which becomes the concept. With practice, we may observe these three phases in the learning process. Each phase blends into the next.

Grammar is particularly suited to awaken moments of healthy consciousness among children. We start with a grammatical conclusion; for example, "The sun is shining." This is a simple fact they have understood many times before. Now we use this fact to understand grammar. We write it on the board. Now they have a conclusion about the sun. This is our starting point.

The next step is to judge how the sun is shining. Is it warm or hot, or as in Norway, far away and cold in the winter? With young children it is always good to be playful; for example, you can ask them how the sun is shining on the horse in the field, or on the mouse in the grass, or on the lion in Africa?

Once you have guided your pupils into making the conclusions and judgments, the next step is to move forward by placing all of those experiences into a meaningful relationship. This is never easy for a teacher. It is tempting to give them a finished product, the right answer, which is a mental image, a statement, or another conclusion. You may want to give them the definition of the sun. For example, we give them a comparison of the sun with a raging ball of fire. How much more creative and powerful may the child`s own concept of the sun be?

The educational question remains, "Are you filling up the children`s consciousness with the right answer or are you allowing them to create their own concept and thereby raising their consciousness? Are you letting them think independently about the sun or are you playing it safe with a scientifically approved conclusion of the sun? You may ask yourself these tough questions in the lesson, in front of the children, and see how creative you are being in the moment. Remember, this is your chance to guide the children into creating their own concepts.

A non-creative method of teaching grammar is to give them the accepted rule for nouns: "A noun is a person, place, or thing." We have remembered that all of our lives because it was on the test the following Friday, probably in the fourth grade English lesson.

The art of guiding children to create their own concept of the noun forces you to continually learn grammar. It is like doing a headstand. You try and retry. Finally you succeed. Your intention should be to develop the lesson so the children discover from each other's conclusions and judgments what their own meaningful context may be. You ask them to put their context into words. By doing so, they raise their consciousness to the level of conceptualization.

You thereby allow the concept of the noun to evolve from within the child. In other words, you let the children tell you what a noun is. Then you repeat the threefold process using verbs. You let them tell you what a verb is. This is very different from learning rules about nouns and verbs that the teacher has dictated.

The real art of grammar is to guide the children into creating their own concept of each part of speech. The rules I share in the workbooks merely point in the right direction; your examples based on the flow of your teaching are much more important. I hope this is helpful to all teachers who are guiding their children in grammatical concept development in grades four through eight.

Teaching Grammar Based on Knowledge of the Human Being

The main goal with teaching is to guide our children into healthy relationships with their thinking and willing between the years of seven and fourteen. At the Waldorf Schools, we base these efforts on the cultivation of their feelings. This is the art of education and it is good to remember that we can fail in this. When children continue to suffer from feelings that tear them apart, their education is failing them. If we notice that children have become skeptics in their feelings and will, their education is not working. They will think one way and act another. This essay provides insight on how to use grammar lessons to help children create a true relationship between their thinking and willing before adolescence.

In his first Waldorf lecture series, Rudolf Steiner introduced a very clear picture of child development. He began with the child´s ability to create mental images. The mental images meet the forces of antipathy and sympathy in her life of feeling and are reflected back towards the past. With these mental images the child creates pictures, and eventually, concepts.

The opposite takes place with mental images that a child creates in her will by observing the world. These images become seeds for the future and are powered by the child`s own sympathy, which is often inspired by the sympathy a teacher shares with her student.

The child's thinking, feeling, and willing work in separate directions. Therefore the art of education is to give the child healthy experiences in which she connects these forces within her feelings. In each lesson we can appeal to both directions in the child´s soul activity. We provide methods for the children to use their antipathy, their ability to be objective in order to create mental images. Later in the lesson, we can use methods that appeal to their sympathy and will, to give nourishment to the other side of their creativity.

Ideal phases in the first nine years of school

In his lectures on education, we find ideal phases in child development that Rudolf Steiner identified and implemented for many years before he started a school. He found four main phases in the first nine years of school: the years before nine, before twelve, before fourteen, and after fourteen. All of his curriculum, educational principles, methods, and psychology are based on these phases in child development. Grammar is one of many subjects Steiner developed along these lines.

Grammar before the age of nine

During the first years of school, before the age of nine, we appeal to the power of imitation in our pupils. We ask them to imitate grammar rather than raising it into their consciousness. By singing songs, reciting poems, playing games, writing words, and hearing stories, they not only learn the structure of the language by imitation, but they also become familiar with the sounds of the language, the way people in their culture speak, as well as how the native speakers relate to each other. The seeds for learning language are set.

We intentionally de-emphasize intellectual stimulus until the age of nine. At that time, some of their life forces are freed from their physical body and become available for conceptualization, the ability to picture the world, and to find meaningful context. Before age nine, we do not include grammar or syntax. We simply speak the mother tongue and foreign languages so the children acquire them as with any other habit.

Grammar before the age of twelve

In the next phase, between the ages of nine and twelve, we no longer teach grammar out of imitation but out of our authority as adults. This is to support the healthy interpenetration of thinking with the child´s will in her life of feelings. One example of how adults fail at this is when moral or intellectual attitudes are forced on children before they can develop their own concepts. All forms of prejudice polarize children.

At the age of nine, the children experience themselves as separated from the world. Childhood fades into the background and they begin to reflect upon who they are. Teaching grammar is an inspiring way to help children grasp these changes productively.

"Between the ninth and tenth years, children go from the level of awareness to self-awareness; they distinguish themselves from the world. At this age, we can begin (gradually, of course) teaching grammar and syntax rules, because the children are reaching a point where they think not only about the world, but also about themselves. As far as speech is concerned, thinking about oneself means not merely being able to speak instinctively, but also being able to apply rational rules in language. It makes no sense, therefore, to teach language with no grammar at all. By avoiding rules altogether, we cannot give children the necessary inner firmness for life's tasks. It is most important to keep in mind that children do not pass willingly from awareness to self-awareness until nine or ten. To teach grammar before then is absolutely irrational." [1]

One guiding method for introducing grammar in the mother tongue and in foreign languages was given in lecture nine of the series entitled "Practical Advice to Teachers." There, Steiner suggested using the way children naturally obtain knowledge: begin with conclusions, then move to judgments of those conclusions, and then build concepts. All of his methods for teaching students before the age of fourteen follow this simple educational principle. This is challenging for every teacher.

He suggested we present activities that create inner enlivenment. The topic may be a raindrop on the car windshield. The teacher states the *conclusions*, "It is raining. It rains." The *judgment w*ould be, "The raindrop falls". And then we lead the children into the *concept*: "The falling raindrop runs down the windshield of the car."

You can move into further activities: "There is lightning; the waterfall is thundering; the boat is sailing". All of these are conclusions. The next step would be to judge these activities: "The lightning is bright; the waterfall is making it hard for me to hear; the boat is sailing downwind." We can also judge the activities by comparing them as questions with statements. What is the difference between, "Is it raining?" and "It is raining."? Is there a difference between, "Is the waterfall thundering?" and "It is thundering!"?

Another method for raising self-awareness through grammar is to analyze simple sentences word for word. Which word comes first? Which word is in the middle of the sentence? Which at the end? How do the words sound? Is anything repeated? Then we may pronounce each syllable of the word, first slowly, then more rapidly. We can ask the children to speak the sentence with intonation so they express feelings in these sentences. The logical structure in the language appears in their judgment and is brought slowly into consciousness.

When we introduce grammar and syntax, we draw it out of the stories and poems they already know. We use familiar sentence structures to tap their memories. This may be supplemented by presenting a new text and asking them to reproduce the content verbally. When teaching a foreign language, we may give them a topic for conversation and then circulate around the classroom to hear how well they are doing.

I introduce grammar to ten-year-olds by using a verb and a corresponding noun as bases: The farmer farms. The dancer dances. I guide the class into creating their own concept of a noun and a verb. Then I ask the question, "What kind of a farmer farms?" or "What kind of a nurse nurses?" This makes them conscious of a new area in grammar. Once they have discovered how the nouns, verbs, and the adjectives work in a sentence, I ask the question, "How does the farmer farm?" This brings them into the power of adverbs. It is less important to know what an adverb is than it is to use adverbs creatively in your writing and your speech. Here the teacher shows them how adverbs enliven their language. You may want to have them practice using adverbs to give people real compliments!

When I introduce prepositions, I work with Steiner's method of moving from conclusion to judgment to concept in the following way. I ask the class for two nouns; for example, the cat and the tree. I write them on the board and ask the class for a verb that may indicate what one of the nouns may be doing. They decide: the cat climbs. Now the challenge is to enter the realm of prepositions giving them many conclusions they can eventually judge. So I play around with the possibilities. Can I say, "The cat climbs under the tree?" Can I ask, "Does the cat sit through the tree?" Is that good English? May I say, "The cat climbs above the tree?" They answer, "Maybe, or maybe not."

 If we use new nouns: the mouse and the pig, we can find a verb; for example, "to run."

Now a multitude of judgments become entertaining: "The cat runs into the pig." "The cat runs after the pig."

Once we are saturated with conclusions and judgments, there is a real need in the classroom to put all of these experiences into a meaningful context. The teacher becomes a guide again and leads the class into a meaningful concept for a preposition.

Steiner suggests that at twelve years of age, children should deal with things that happen in real life: writing letters and business correspondence and recounting things that have happened to them, rather than writing free essays. In foreign language teaching, you can give them orders they need to carry out. This challenges them to act rather than reflect upon the language. It engages their will.

Grammar before the age of fourteen

In the twelfth year, we should be able to introduce a large part of the grammar of the mother tongue and of the foreign language. Whatever is introduced one year should be repeated the following year at a new level, giving all of the children a new chance to gain confidence in their skills. Using a good sense of humor and appealing to the intellect in a new way each year, the goal is to help the teenagers know that they know grammar. This good feeling depends on our authority as teachers, which is displayed in our methods, our principles, our ability to see them as human beings, and our ability to follow their learning processes. This can be done economically, meaning devoid of activities that bear no lifelong fruits. Teens need to learn according to their capacities.

Free rendering through conversation of a passage they have read is a good method. You ask them to repeat the passage in their own words. Another method is to discuss a subject in the mother tongue that they follow in their feelings and thoughts and let them express it in the foreign language. Thus they learn to think in each language.

Remember that grammar should be developed independently. Steiner suggests, "When you carry on grammar and syntax with the children you will, then, have to make up sentences specifically to illustrate this or that grammatical rule. But you will have to see to it that the children do not write down these sentences illustrating grammatical rules. Instead of being put down in their workbooks they should be worked on; they come into being but they are not preserved. This procedure contributes enormously to the economical use of your lessons, particularly those for foreign languages, for in this way the children absorb the rules in their feelings and after awhile drop the examples. If they are allowed to write down the examples, they absorb the form of the example too strongly, whereas for the teaching of grammar the examples ought to be dispensable; they should not be carefully written down in workbooks, for only the rule should finally remain. So it is good for the living language, actual speaking, to use exercises and reading passages as just described, and on the other hand to let the children formulate their own thoughts in the foreign language, using more the kind of subject that crops up in daily life. For grammar, however, you use sentences that from the start you intend the children to forget and therefore you do not do what is always a help in memorizing: write them down. For all the activity involved in teaching the children grammar and syntax with the help of sentences takes place in living conclusions; it should not descend into the dreamlike state of habitual actions but continue to play in fully conscious life." [2]

You can present your own examples to the class one day; the next day you ask them to create their own examples. The examples given in textbooks need not be repeated. As you can see, any teacher of languages needs to relearn the grammar of that language. No matter what level of grammar you have obtained at college, continual learning is needed in order to reach the children in the classroom each day.

When new children enter the class or you take over a new class, find out what they know and what they do not know in grammar. You have to close those gaps. When they reach the point of being able to understand grammar and syntax in one language, they are then able to enliven their knowledge of another language.

Grammar after the age of fourteen

Fourteen-year-olds at a Waldorf School will have learned plenty of grammar. By now they can use grammar to improve their writing style, their reading comprehension, and their ability to speak out of inner freedom. They can now reach for the next level of *knowing that they know* and thereby experience a new sense of confidence.

Our goal has been to use the grammar lessons to allow the teenager to develop self-awareness based on what she already knows in the structure of the language. This self-awareness has been developed with methods that give the teen the ability to create independent concepts. She has done this in many other subjects at the school. In this way, she develops her moral life within her feelings. When she enters puberty, these feelings will help her further develop her intellect and further awaken her moral feelings: all of this according to her own spontaneity. Her feelings will flow back into her intellect. There will be healthy integration in her sympathy and antipathy as she discovers how life works in the world at large and in other people. Her understanding of grammar helps her learn from more complicated texts about nature, science, economics, politics, and all other subjects that interest her. She is ready to face the many challenges that will appear as she navigates through her life.

Sources

1. Rudolf Steiner, Lecture on "Problems of Education," Lecture Six, London, November 19, 1922, page 100.
2. Rudolf Steiner, "Practical Advice To Teachers" Lecture Nine, Stuttgart, August 30, 1919, page 133.

Weekly Exercises

The Teenage Edge

Every child has its own learning style and its own level of English. In a classroom you may have children from different schools with very different experiences in the English language. How do we bring them all up to speed? How can we reach them all in productive learning processes that take place on a regular basis? Can the process be interesting for all of the children, no matter where they stand in their learning? My answer is, "Absolutely!"

Every teacher can create a twenty-minute exercise each week that all of the children enjoy and find productive. The goal is to provide opportunities where the children experience that they are learning regularly. The parents and children will relax when they know that there is a specified, weekly learning process for teaching grammar, spelling, etc., each week on the same day. They will all look forward to it. Let us look at the framework of the exercise. First of all, the teacher gives the children a fair, but challenging weekly assignment to prepare for the day the exercise takes place. Choose one day each week for the whole school year. Then show them how they can prepare. If the content is *spelling new vocabulary correctly*, advise them to write each word five times. They can do this in the lesson or at home. When the day comes for the exercise include the content, in this case spelling vocabulary words, in a new and larger context so everyone is challenged in the twenty minute period of the exercise. Let them know that the only mistakes that count are the content they were supposed to learn that week, but that they must complete the whole exercise in class and be willing to make mistakes. It is very important for children to feel comfortable making mistakes. We all make mistakes every day in real life, why not at school? Of course the goal is to learn from your mistakes and not repeat them. Children who learn from their mistakes make significant progress.

The challenging part of the exercise with vocabulary words may be dictating a couple of paragraphs that include the new words. You may read the paragraphs and ask them to write them. The only mistakes that count are the words they were asked to prepare. When the teacher corrects the results at home, he sees how much progress the children are making. Give them a result. I write either excellent, good, or retake. The retake is to give them a consequence for not having prepared the exercise. I also ask the children who were not in the lesson that day to do the retake. Those who have not learned enough, retake the exercise. Be creative with the content of the exercise and change it according to the learning you are providing. You will be surprised how much English they will have learned after some months with weekly exercises. The learning results are accumulative. They will know that you know how well they are learning and so will the parent.

Fourth Grade Key Concepts by Chapter

The following key concepts point you in the right direction for guiding the children into creating their own concepts of how the English language works.

Writing Sentences and Paragraphs

A sentence has a subject and a verb.

The first word is always capitalized, and the sentence ends with punctuation: a period (.), a question mark (?), or an exclamation point (!).

A paragraph has two or more sentences about the same topic. The first sentence introduces the paragraph and is indented five spaces.

Nouns and Verbs with the Same Bases

The farmer farms.

Verbs

Verbs (v) exist in time. They are expressed in many tenses or times. Among others, there are the present tense, the past tense, and the future tense.

A verb expresses action.

Nouns

Nouns (n), pronouns, and articles do not exist in a stream of time. Therefore verbs and nouns are polarities in the English language. A language without verbs would show no action. A language without nouns would have no backbone.

Nouns are always plural or singular.

After they have formed their concept, you can guide the children into understanding the classic rule: "A noun is a person, place, or thing."

Articles

Articles (a) determine whether a noun is definite or indefinite. A definite article makes the noun specific: "the cat." The indefinite article leaves the noun wide open. It may be any example of the noun: "a cat."

Pronouns

In modern English the word pronoun (p) means roughly "for the name." Pronouns replace nouns to improve the flow of the language.

Adjectives

Between the polarities of verbs and nouns, we have adjectives (adj.); for example, red, sour, sharp, sweet, sticky, happy, or lost. Adjectives express, even more specifically, how something is experienced. They move back and forth between nouns and verbs. Often they define the atmosphere of the noun and action. They express feelings. They tell us how the world really is. They tell us about the person who acts, about the action itself, and about our senses.

Adverbs

Adverbs (adv.) add especially to the verbs. Adverbs express the quality of verbs, adjectives, and other adverbs.

Prepositions

Prepositions (prep.) place the subject of the sentence and the action in relation to another object. The prepositional phrase contains a preposition, its object, and usually an article.

Connectives/Conjunctions

In astronomy, a conjunction (conj.) is the meeting or passing of two or more heavenly bodies in the same degree of the zodiac. In English grammar, it is the meeting of two or more sentences, clauses, phrases, or words in the same degree of the language.

Connectives are also called conjunctions: words that join sentences, clauses, phrases, or words. Conjunctions create relationships.

Interjections

Interjections (interj.) are words or phrases that show strong feelings.

Simple and Compound Sentences

Simple sentences have one noun and one verb. Compound sentences are two or more sentences joined by a conjunction.

Irregular Verbs

Here is a method I have used to develop irregular verbs. Every week, give the children three verbs to learn by heart in all three tenses. They learn the present tense form, the past tense form, and the perfect tense form: become, became, become.

That gives them nine words on the dictation they must spell correctly. You dictate whole sentences so they must practice writing English freely, without fear of making mistakes. On the dictation they are held accountable only for the nine verbs they learned by heart that week, in preparation for the dictation.

Collect the dictation and correct it, noting their results. Write down the correct answers for them. If more than thirty percent of the irregular verbs are wrong, give them a retake the next day. If more than thirty percent are wrong on the retake, give them a retake in the next break or at the end of the lesson. Continue with retakes until they write all nine verb forms correctly.

This method allows children to develop their own method of learning how to spell, even if they have serious learning challenges. It takes place regularly, and the children enjoy the consistency in their learning process.

The Use of Will and Shall

There is confusion about when to use *will* and *shall* with the first person singular and plural pronouns: *I* and *we*. The standard American and British rule is that they are interchangeable, but *shall* is rarely used in American English.

Here are examples of how *shall* is used in American English. It is required in legal documents and binding contracts. *Shall* is also used in prose such as in *The Gettysburg Address*. It is found in songs such as *We Shall Overcome*. It is used to show formality such as, *"Shall I buy tickets for the game?"* or *"Shall we dance?"*

Fourth Grade Games and Drawings

The Teenage Edge

Children who love to play will also love to work. Therefore, it is good for the children when the teacher creates learning games. I will share some of mine with you so that you can develop your own.

Verb Conjugation Game

It is fun to ask the children to act out a verb conjugation in front of the class. They need five kids to fill all eight roles. The group of five decides who represents I, you, he, she, it, we, you, and they. The game is to present situations where any combination of these pronouns is acted out. The children in their seats guess which conjugation it is (singular or plural) and what the situation is. Those who guess properly come forward and replace the original five once they have completed all eight situations.

Once the class is confident and all have mastered the game, split them into teams of five and time how fast they can present all eight situations. The group taking as little time as possible with eight clearly-presented situations, wins.

Drawing Exercise 1

Let the children draw the actions taken in the game and then compare their results.

Verb Tense Game

A verb tense game may begin with the teacher asking one child to act out a verb in front of the class and letting the others guess what the verb is: for example, shoveling, zipping, cutting, dancing, hoeing, counting, and so forth. All of the pantomimed actions take place in the present.

When that child is finished, she sits on a stool in front of the class and is asked to be silent while the next one gets up to act out a new verb. Now the child on the stool can guess what the other child is acting out. The teacher names the stool *the stool from the past.* When the child sitting on the stool guesses correctly, the child that did the pantomime gets to sit on *the stool from the past.* She moves from the present into the past. A new child stands before the class and pantomimes another verb. When the child on the *stool from the past* guesses correctly, the teacher asks the child in the present tense role, "What did you do?" The child answers in the past tense and then sits down on *the stool of the past.*

Repeat the game until the children are clear about the process, then move it into the future tense.

Another stool is set before the class on the other side of the child that pantomimes in the present. This is the *stool of the future.* The teacher asks the child that steps forward to pantomime, to whisper what he will do; for example, "I will saw." The future is hidden within the child and the teacher. It is unknown. It is a matter of willpower. The action will appear in the next moment from the hidden intention. "Do it!" says the teacher. The child stands up and carries out the future intention as a present action. The other children forget to raise their hands and shout out, "He saws!" The child that *sawed* sits on *the stool of the future.* Silence. The teacher pretends he has not been paying attention and then suddenly asks again, "What did he do?" The class answers in chorus, "He sawed!"

Teachers, students, and parents can create variations on the game by making new rules and setting new goals.

Drawing 2

Ask the children to draw the activities of the game in all three tenses. The drawing can be expanded to include three human figures within circles: one in the present, one in the past, and one in the future. Let the children draw arrows from circle to circle according to the actions of the verb tenses they choose to work with.

A Pronoun Game

In front of the class, while playing out the role they chose spontaneously, the child will know if she is in the first person, second person, or third person singular or plural. You set the stage for the scene, and the students will quickly make their own local dialogue.

For example:

"Hello, I am Jeff. So where are you from?"

"I am from Scranton."

"And where is this other guy from?"

"He is from Peckville."

"And where does the MG driver live?"

"She is from Dickson City."

" I like the shirt you have on. Where did you get it?"

"It is from Taylor."

"Do both of you know Giovanni?"

"Yes, we are from Jessup."

"And where do the Lombardos live?"

"They are from Old Forge."

At that moment two other children walk in.

"Hello. We are late. Would you like to go swimming?"

They greet each other and walk off arm in arm.

The Teacher's Manual for Three Workbooks

A Preposition Game

Find two nouns; for example, the dog and the cat. Place a list of prepositions between them. You can either let them speak or write the examples on the blackboard.

    The dog   the cat.

            between

            above

            behind

            near

Now add the verb: runs

    The dog runs   the cat.

            between

            above

            behind

            near

Ask the pupils to pantomime the dog and the cat according to the verb and the prepositions. This will give them more judgment of how the prepositions work and increase their feeling for the language.

Then change the nouns, the prepositions, and the verbs.

Fourth Grade Workbook
List of Grammatical Content

The Teenage Edge

The Verb Conjugation Chart, Figure 1	page 9
The Pronoun Chart, Figure 2	page 11
The Verb "to be"	page 17
The Verb "to have"	page 21
The Progressive Tense	page 26
Irregular Verbs in the Past and Present Perfect Tenses	page 32-37
Incomplete Irregular Verb List	page 35
The Future Tense	page 38
Adjectives	page 46
List of Adjectives	page 48
Adverbs	page 49
Adverbs of Compound Words	page 51
Adverbs of Manner	page 52
Adverbs of Time	page 53
Adverbs of Frequency	page 54
Adverbs of Place	page 55
Adverbs "To what extent?"	page 55
Adverbs of Degree	page 56
Adverb Exercises	page 57
Nouns	page 58
Common Nouns	page 58
Proper Nouns	page 58
Compound Nouns Forming Word Groups	page 58

The Teacher's Manual for Three Workbooks

Forming Plurals with Irregular Nouns .... page 59

Irregular Plurals .... page 62

Articles .... page 65

Pronouns .... page 68

Personal Pronouns .... page 68

Reflexive Pronouns .... page 70

Interrogative Pronouns .... page 72

Prepositions .... page 75

Connectives/Conjunctions .... page 79

Simple and Compound Sentences .... page 83

Interjections .... page 86

Numbers .... page 88

Punctuation .... page 90

Capitalization .... page 92

Writing a Personal Letter .... page 94

Fifth Grade
Key Concepts By Chapter

The Teenage Edge

Parts of speech   (Pages 5 - 8)

The exercise of identifying parts of speech in a sentence is not a goal in itself. It merely gives the children practice in knowing how the words work in the sentence. They learn to define how the word works. Their concept of how the words relate to each other in a sentence grows through practice.

Direct and indirect speech   (Pages 9 - 12)

Here you have two types of speech that can be presented with the method I have described which starts with conclusions, develops judgments, and builds concepts in the learning process. Begin with either direct or indirect speech. Then develop the other. Once the children are comfortable with both types of speech, you may compare them. This is part of the judgment phase. When they are able to define each, you have helped them generate the concept. The work becomes more complicated when you introduce the use of punctuation in both types of speech.

Active voice and passive voice   (Pages 12 - 16)

Here children discover how the subject of the sentence actively uses the verb, compared with the subject being passively influenced by the verb. The concepts of subject and object evolve according to the methods you use. A difference in the meaning of the sentences also appears in the children`s consciousness. Here we need to take our time so they may become confident of their insight and use of the concepts.

Verbs in complex tenses   (Pages 17 - 46)

Helping verbs and auxiliary verbs

In the workbook I call these verbs *helping verbs* to keep things simple. In grammar, ten helping verbs are known as modal auxiliaries: can, could, may, might, must, ought to, shall, should, will, and would. These do not change form when used. They help the main verb express particular meanings: certainty, ability, possibility, permission, or the lack of these.

    Ability: I can do it. Can't I do it?

The Teacher's Manual for Three Workbooks

Possibility: I could do it if you showed me. I couldn't do it; you did not show me. I might be able to win. I might not.

Permission: May I go there? You may not.

Certainty: You must leave. We shall help.
We ought to help her.

The other helping verbs, *to be, to have, do, need to*, and *used to*, change form according to the tense used in the sentence.

Tenses in time

Helping children develop their sense of time is always a great experience in the classroom. For eleven-year-olds it has an awakening affect. They have experienced time for many years, but now it becomes more conscious.

As a teacher you will notice how differently the children comprehend the tenses. Some pick it up quickly, and others need a lot of time to enter the tenses, and thereby develop the concepts. Spend time on this. Once the children comprehend the tense and can use it effectively, they can also speak and write in the correct moment of time. This improves their reading comprehension because they more easily understand authors who describe events in many different times.

The more complicated verb forms present new aspects of the three basic tenses: present, past, and future. They cross in and out of the various relationships in time; for example, *"Yesterday I cut wood."* Here I return to the action as it happened. This is the past tense.

Perfect tenses

If I say, *" I had cut wood."* I return to the time in the past when the action was already finished. This is the past perfect tense, a finished picture projected into the past. We reflect upon the picture with our thoughts.

In the perfect tense, something has happened in the present. The action is within a finished picture in the present. Therefore we use the helping verb, *to have* in the present tense. The perfect tense, *"I have cut wood."* is in the present, but it is a completed action.

The past perfect tense, *"I had cut wood."* is in the past and is a completed action. Something has happened in the past. The past perfect tense is formed by *had* and a past participle. It is used with an action that is concluded before a certain time in the past. The action could also take place before another action.

In the future perfect tense, the sentence is in the future and is a completed action. *"I will have cut wood."* Something will have happened in the future. In this case, I will have cut wood in the future. Formed by the future tense of "to have" and a past perfect participle, it indicates an action that will be completed before a certain time in the future or before another action in the future. This tense is often used with the prepositions *by* and *that*.

Notice that the perfect tense, the past perfect tense, and the future perfect tenses are reflections. We are using verb tenses to think about what has happened.

Progressive tenses

The *present perfect progressive tense* expresses the duration of an action up to the present. The action is still continuing at the moment of speaking. It may continue into the future. *I have been fishing.*

The *past perfect progressive tense* is formed by 'had been' and the present participle form of the verb. *I had been fishing.* It is used in two ways:

1. To express the duration of an action up to a certain time in the past.
   When I got to the slopes, the lift had been running for half an hour.

2. To express the present perfect progressive in reported speech.
   I asked him what he had been doing since he arrived in Scranton.
   He told me that he had been swimming in the creek.

The future perfect progressive tense is formed by the future tense of *have* and *been* and the present participle form of the verb. It is used to express the duration of an action up to a certain time in the future.

By tomorrow, I will have understood the complex verb forms.

Adverbs (Pages 47 - 51)

The definition of adverbs states that they modify verbs, adverbs, and adjectives. When your pupils have created their own concept of what adverbs do in the sentence, you can use the definition of an adverb to remind them of how adverbs may be used. How often do children decide to use more adverbs to modify their verbs, adverbs, and adjectives? Once again, the goal is to guide the children into using adverbs more consciously and vividly in their language.

The use of *good* and *well*.

Both *good* and *well* can act as adverbs, though *good* is not preferred. The following sentences show the difference in their use.

If someone asks how the tennis game was, we would say, "It went well." *Well* modifies the verb *went*. We do not say, "The game went good," because *good* is not commonly used as an adverb. We could say, "It was a good game." Here *good* is used properly as an adjective.

"He did a good job," not "He did good." We do say, "He did well."

Where to place the adverbs

In the fifth grade, it is most important to engage the children in using adverbs powerfully. The following rules on placement are more important for the sixth grade, but the teacher should be aware of it in the fifth grade work.

Adverbs of manner are placed behind the direct object or verb.

> Examples: slowly, carefully, fast, purposely, and so on.
> He climbed over the tree quickly.
> He climbed quickly.

Adverbs of place go behind the direct object or verb.

> Examples: below, under, after, before, and so on.
> I brought it here.
> She walked there.

Adverbs of time are usually placed at the end of the sentence.

> Examples: now, tomorrow, recently, and so on.
> I saw her walk down my street recently.
> We will go there tomorrow.

Adverbs of frequency are placed directly before the main verb.

> Examples: seldom, always, usually, and so on.
> I often go swimming after school.
> I always say, "Thank You."

Relative adverbs: where, when, and why

Relative adverbs introduce a clause. For example:

> He knew where the storm came from.
> Toot when you are ready?
> Will you honk when you are ready?.

The use of will and shall

There is confusion about when to use *will* and *shall* with the first person singular and plural pronouns: *I* and *we*. The standard American and British rule is that they are interchangeable, but *shall* is rarely used in American English. In American English, *shall* is used in legal documents and binding contracts. *Shall* is also used in prose such as in *The Gettysburg Address.* It is found in songs such as *We Shall Overcome*. It is used to show formality such as, "*Shall I buy us a ticket for the game?* " and "*Shall we dance*?"

Conjunctions (Pages 53 -53)

A compound sentence is made of two independent sentences that can stand alone. They are connected by coordinating conjunctions. Always use a comma before the coordinating conjunctions: *for, and, nor, but, or, yet*, and *so*.

For instance: We ran to the beach, and we jumped into the surf.

Interjections (Page 54)

We want our pupils to use their interjections so well that they have a powerful effect on the sentence. The concept you can develop with them is to be aware of how the interjection works in the sentence. Does it emphasize their statement? Does it act as a command? How are they responding to the statement of another person: by protest, as an answer, or in confirmation? Will they use a single word or a phrase? How often should they use interjections in a story?

Pronouns (Pages 55 - 65)

If someone tells you that a pronoun replaces a noun, you receive an abstract definition. If they say a pronoun replaces a person, place, or thing you have a more detailed abstraction to remember. If they give a random list of pronouns such as we, that, much, many, anything, who, whose, and me, you receive another abstraction, now in the form of a list. How much more interesting is it for you to actually know how to use those pronouns in sentences. That requires an effort on your part to learn the grammar of pronouns again. In order to use those random pronouns in sentences, you need to know how they work in sentences. That requires even more effort. This shows the difference between observing abstractions and actually learning how the pronouns work in order to teach children how to discover that for themselves.

Use punctuation (commas, parentheses, dashes) to set off non-restrictive/parenthetical elements

These concepts (found as Grammar Rules 24 and 25 and Exercise 58 in the 5th Grade English Workbook), are important for the teacher's understanding, but not essential for the children in the 5th grade. Children need to improve their use of commas in the fifth grade, but I would save the concept development until the sixth grade. At that time, the logic involved concerning types of clauses and when to use commas becomes a good challenge for twelve-year-olds. In the fifth grade focus on the use of commas with the relative pronouns *that* and *which*.

A parenthetical element is additional information that is used to clarify the meaning of the sentence. It will be found as a word, a phrase, or a clause and needs to have the proper punctuation. Commas are most commonly used, but dashes and parentheses are also acceptable. In the fifth grade we only focus on the commas.

The parenthetical elements may be restrictive or non-restrictive. Restrictive elements are necessary for the meaning of the sentence. They are most often introduced by *that*. We do not use commas to enclose restrictive elements. There is no comma before *that* and after well in the following example because we do not use a comma before and after restrictive clauses.

> The dappled, grey horse that I know well came up to great me.

Non-restrictive elements are not necessary for the meaning of the sentence. *Which* is commonly used to indicate a non-restrictive element. The clause introduced by *which* is enclosed by commas.

> My lawn, which has grown quickly, will be cut tomorrow.

Prepositions (Pages 66 -72)

Prepositions show the relationship between nouns in the sentence. In the fifth grade, the children can practice using many different prepositions and thereby become confident in which preposition works well in their sentences.

Nouns (Pages 73 -77)

This is a huge chapter where you want to build vocabulary as you work and guide them into knowing how the nouns work in the sentences as subjects and objects. Classifying nouns is not so important at this age; it is more valuable to increase the joy of learning new nouns and finding the verbs, phrases, clauses, and the other parts of speech that enable the child to express her message.

Adjectives (Pages 78 -86)

The first rule to remember is that you never separate one adjective from its noun:

> The warm sand fell across her toes.
> (Here we do not use a comma to separate warm from sand.)

When there is more than one adjective used before a noun, it may be necessary to separate them with a comma.

> For instance: She threw her towel over her wet, scared dog.

These are coordinate adjectives in that you can reverse them, or put 'and' between them without detracting from the meaning:

She threw her towel over her scared, wet dog.

She threw her towel over her wet and scared dog.

All three ways make equal sense. In two of them a comma is used.

Ordering cumulative adjectives according to conventional patterns

Commas are not used with cumulative adjectives; for instance, Zora enjoyed her root beer float after school. You cannot change the order of *root beer float* or put *and* between the adjectives because to do so would change the accepted flow of the language.

> Here are more examples:
>
> I have tickets to a Boston Red Sox game.
>
> We watch Saturday night movies.
>
> The seven talented Canadian hockey players have joined our team.

This is the order for the placement of cumulative adjectives:

> Number (sixteen, many, a)
>
> Opinion (useful, stylish)
>
> Size (huge, small)
>
> Age (new, ancient)
>
> Shape (round, square)
>
> Color (blue, green)
>
> Origin (American, Sears)
>
> Material (plastic, cotton)
>
> Purpose (fun, play)

Once again, save the conscious ordering of adjectives for the sixth grade. When you notice that the students' sentences lose their meaning due to the wrong placement of adjectives, you can point it out to them.

Using the relative adjectives *where*, *when*, *why*.

These adjectives introduce clauses.

Punctuation (Pages 87 - 92)

Review from last year

It is important to review all of the punctuation and capitalization rules introduced in the Fourth Grade Grammar Workbook. The students need to feel confident in using these rules. The following rules were introduced in the fourth grade book. Find interesting ways to review these with your class.

The fourth grade punctuation and capitalization rules include:

1. The period is used to bring a thought to a stop.
2. The question mark tells that a question has been asked.
3. The exclamation point is used to show great feeling or emotion.
4. The comma is used between words in a series of three or more items and is put before the conjunction that links them.
5. All proper nouns are capitalized.
6. The capital letter is used in the greeting and closing of a letter.
7. Capital letters are used with abbreviations.
8. The first letter in a sentence is capitalized.
9. Capital letters are used in quotations.
10. The names of people, proper nouns, days of the week, months, places, organizations, and businesses are capitalized.
11. The punctuation used when writing a personal letter.

The new punctuation and capitalization concepts you teach are on pages 87 to 92 in the 5th grade book.

Fifth Grade Games, Drawings, And Memory Exercises

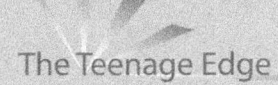 The Teenage Edge

Complex tenses game

In grade five, we learn the more complicated tenses in a game. Two children stand in front of the class. One sits in the "stool of the future." The other stands behind it. The first one says, " I will paint." (future tense) The child behind says,

"Soon he will have painted a complete painting." (future perfect tense) The first child stands up and pantomimes painting and says, "I paint." (present) Then he stops painting and the children in the class as a chorus say, "Now he has painted completely." (present perfect tense)

The first child sits on the stool of the past and says, "I painted." The other child stands behind the "stool of the past" and says, "Awhile ago, I had already painted completely." (past perfect tense) Then the teacher can ask questions that require the pupils to use the various tenses.

Drawing exercises

After you play the game, let the children draw it. For example, draw the actions three times in all three tenses. Color the picture in their memory from the past, red and the picture of the willpower intention in the future, blue. Use a separate color for the moment (perhaps green). They can write down examples of verbs in columns below that represent the past, present, and future.

Remember not to draw such a picture in advance of the game. The game provides experiences for the children. These experiences are the basis for conclusions that lead to judgments and finally to concepts which the children have created within their learning process.

The drawing can be expanded to include three human figures within circles: one in the present, one in the past, and one in the future. Let the children draw arrows from circle to circle according to the actions of the verb tenses they choose to work with.

Drawing exercises of complex tenses

Make a graphic overview by drawing a horizontal line with three points high-lighted: one is the future, the next the present, and the third the past. Then draw three vertical lines that pass through the highlighted points. Name them the future perfect, the present perfect, and the past perfect tenses.

Some pupils will use different colors for the different tenses. Some will draw different events taking place. You will be inspired by the way they interpret their understanding visually.

Memory exercises

No matter where you are in the workbook, you may create a memory exercise for the pupils. They can practice memorizing in the classroom. You can ask them to memorize as homework.

Drawing or painting a topic is an introductory phase in developing memory. If you have worked on the present, past, and future tenses in the lesson, give them a piece of paper and let them freely draw their picture of those tenses. You will be inspired by the way they interpret their understanding visually. Then they move forward in their memorization.

Suggested topics for memorization are complex verb tenses, relative pronouns, and new adverbs.

List Of Content In The Fifth Grade Workbook

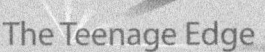

Figure 1	Active and passive voice	page 13
Figure 2	Irregular verb lists	pages 17 – 22
Figure 3	Irregular verb endings with sounds	page 23
Figure 4	Future tense with will and shall	page 26
Figure 5	Verb matrix	page 37
Figure 6	Multiple tenses with "to speak"	page 38
Figure 7	Multiple tenses with irregular verbs	page 39
Figure 8	Active and passive voice	page 41
Figure 9	Nominative and objective pronouns	page 55
Figure 10	Nominative and objective pronouns together	page 56
Figure 11	Adjectives using more and most	page 79
Figure 12	Irregular adjectives	pages 80, 81
Figure 13	Writing letters: personal and business	pages 95 to 96

Fifth Grade Workbook List of Grammatical Content

Parts of speech	page 5
Direct and indirect speech	page 9
Active and passive voice	page 12
Verbs in complex tenses	pages 17 – 47
Irregular verb list	pages 17 – 22

The Teacher's Manual for Three Workbooks

Irregular verbs by endings, patterns, and sounds	page 23
Helping verbs	page 24
Complicated tenses	page 24
Simple present tense	page 25
Simple past tense	page 25
Future tense	page 26
Contractions with *will* and *shall*	page 26
Present progressive	page 27
Past progressive	page 28
Future progressive	page 29
Present perfect	page 32
Future perfect tense	page 33
Present perfect progressive	page 34
Past perfect progressive	page 35
Future perfect progressive	page 36
Verb tense matrix	page 37
Multiple tenses	page 38
Active and passive tense	page 41
Verbs with indirect and direct objects	page 46
Adverbs	page 47
Comparison of adverbs	page 48
Where, when, and why	page 49
Well and good	page 50
Conjunctions	page 52
Conjunctions in compound sentences	page 53
Interjections	page 54
Nominative and objective pronouns	page 55

Relative pronouns: who, whom for people	page 57
Whose	page 58
Which for animals	page 59
Which for things	page 59
Who for animals	page 60
That	page 61
That in objective case	page 62
That after indefinite pronouns	page 62
That after *anything*	page 63
That after *much*	page 63
Which, that, who	page 64
That with no commas	page 65
Prepositional phrases	page 66
Prepositions	page 68
Nouns: common, plural, foreign	page 73
Collective nouns	page 74
Possessive nouns	page 75
Adjectives	page 78
Adjectives with commas	page 85
Adjectives in the correct order	page 85
Punctuation	page 87 – 91
Frequently confused words	page 93
Writing letters	page 95

List of Grammar Rules

Grammar Rule 1	Passive voice in three tenses	page 12
Grammar Rule 2	Helping verb "will"	page 24
Grammar Rule 3	Will and shall	page 24
Grammar Rule 4	Simple past tense	page 25
Grammar Rule 5	Simple past tense	page 26
Grammar Rule 6	Future tense with will	page 26
Grammar Rule 7	Present progressive tense	page 27
Grammar Rule 8	Past progressive tense	page 28
Grammar Rule 9	Future progressive tense	page 29
Grammar Rule 10	Present perfect tense	page 31
Grammar Rule 11	Past perfect tense	page 32
Grammar Rule 12	Future perfect tense	page 33
Grammar Rule 13	Present perfect progressive tense	page 34
Grammar Rule 14	Past perfect progressive tense	page 35
Grammar Rule 15	Future perfect progressive tense	page 36
Grammar Rule 16	Active and passive voice in multiple tenses	page 41
Grammar Rule 17	Verbs with indirect and direct object	page 46
Grammar Rule 18	Commas with compound sentences	page 53
Grammar Rule 19	Who and whom for people	page 57
Grammar Rule 20	Which and that	page 59
Grammar Rule 21	Using who for animals	page 60
Grammar Rule 22	That	page 61
Grammar Rule 23	That after indefinite pronouns	page 62
Grammar Rule 24	Which, that, and who	page 64
Grammar Rule 25	Who	page 66
Grammar Rule 26	Phrases with prepositions	page 66

Grammar Rule 27	Collective nouns	page 74
Grammar Rule 28	Nouns with plural verbs	page 74
Grammar Rule 29	Nouns with two subjects joined by and	page 74
Grammar Rule 30	Singular nouns add apostrophe	page 75
Grammar Rule 31	Possessive nouns that end with "s"	page 75
Grammar Rule 32	Find the plural form first	page 75
Grammar Rule 33	Plural nouns end in s, add apostrophe	page 76
Grammar Rule 34	Plural noun does not end in s, add apostrophe and s	page 76
Grammar Rule 35	Adjectives – doubling rule	page 78
Grammar Rule 36	Two syllable adjective with more or most	page 79
Grammar Rule 37	Commas never separate an adjective from its noun	page 86
Grammar Rule 38	Commas with multiple adjectives	page 86
Grammar Rule 39	The order of adjectives	page 86
Grammar Rule 40	Articles as adjectives	page 86

List of Punctuation Rules

Punctuation rules A	Writing dialogue and direct speech	page 89
Punctuation Rule 1	Quotations around what people say	page 89
Punctuation Rule 2	Double quotations marks	page 89
Punctuation Rule 3	Ending punctuation marks inside quotation marks	page 89
Punctuation Rule 4	Capitalizing first word spoken	page 90
Punctuation Rule 5	Tags	page 90
Punctuation Rule 6	Sentences that continue	page 90
Punctuation Rule 7	Exclamation marks	page 90
Punctuation Rule 8	Semi-colons	page 91
Punctuation Rule 9	New paragraphs	page 91
Punctuation Rule 10	Commas separate items	page 91

The Teacher's Manual for Three Workbooks

Punctuation Rule 11	Commas indicate direct speech	page 92
Punctuation Rule 12	Commas with tag questions	page 92
Punctuation Rule 13	Commas with interjections	page 92
Punctuation Rule 14	Commas with titles of works	page 92

List of Spelling Rules

Spelling Rule 1	Contractions of will	page 27
Spelling Rule 2	From y to i in two syllable adjective comparisons	page 79
Spelling Rule 3	Words ending in ow in adjective comparisons	page 79

List of Tests

Test 1	Verbs	page 42
Test 2	Irregular verbs	page 45
Test 3	Adverbs	page 51
Test 4	Prepositions	page 70

The Sixth To Eighth Grade Key Concepts By Chapter

The Teenage Edge

Suggestions for the sixth grade

The key concepts for the sixth grade are developed to raise self-awareness through grammar. Each year it is important to begin with a review of all of the topics you covered the previous year. Use new methods to do this. Take whatever amount of time your class needs.

By reviewing, you allow the pupils to remember and to learn again the relationships among the words. You may develop key concepts by analyzing simple sentences word for word. Which word comes first in the sentence? Which word is in the middle of the sentence? Which is at the end? What does the word do in the sentence? Does it act as an adjective, adverb, or a noun? You develop the logical structure in the language so your pupils once again become consciousness of the grammar.

Do not plan on covering this entire workbook in the sixth grade. Here are my suggestions as to when to cover which topics. Some topics are repeated in the sixth, seventh, and eighth grades. Others are repeated in the seventh and eighth grades. It is up to you. Use my suggestions to create your own plan.

Types of sentences and word positioning   (Pages 8-11)

There are four basic sentence structures: simple sentences, compound sentences, complex sentences, and compound-complex sentences. What are the differences?

Simple sentences have one or more subjects and one or more verbs. Compound sentences are two or more sentences joined by a conjunction. That may be enough for the sixth grade. If so, continue with the other types of sentences and word positioning in the seventh grade.

Types of sentences and word positioning	6th	7th	8th
Simple sentences	x	x	X
Compound sentences	x	x	X
Complex sentences		x	X
Compound-complex sentences		x	X
The position of nouns		x	X
The position of adjectives		x	X

Parts of speech (Pages 14 - 16)

In the sixth grade, I would keep the review of the parts of speech simple. Restrict it to categories you have already covered well. Recognizing the parts of speech should give the pupils a good feeling.

I do not review articles or interjections in this workbook. Remember that the key concepts concerning articles were covered in the *English Workbook for Fourth Grade.* Interjections were covered in the workbooks for the fourth grade and the fifth Grade.

Clauses 1 (Pages 19-37)

Clauses are a major part of the concept work in this workbook. Teach them well. Repeat and repeat and repeat so the pupils create their concepts anew. Once they get it, repeat again. This is very powerful. Knowledge accumulates.

Build the work year by year as I suggest in the table below.

Clauses 1	6th	7th	8th
Independent clauses	x	x	X
Dependent clauses	x	x	X
Complex sentences	x	x	X
Relative pronouns introduce relative clauses	x	x	X
Relative adverbs introduce relative clauses		x	X
Adjective clauses		x	X
Noun clauses		x	X
Adverb clauses		x	X
Conditional clauses		x	X

Verbs (Pages 46-59)

In the *English Workbook for Fifth Grade,* you taught the verb tenses thoroughly. Re-develop those concepts and even redo some of the exercises to refresh your pupil's memories. To prepare for this, reread the *Verbs in Complex Tenses* section of the chapter, *Fifth Grade Key Concepts By Chapter on pages 27-34 of this teaching manual.*

Transitive and intransitive verbs, verbs with prepositions, special finite verbs, and infinitives are the new concepts to cover in the sixth grade. Examples of these are on pages 46 to 48 in the workbook.

Verbs	6th	7th	8th
The verb matrix	X	X	X
Active and passive voice	X	X	X
Transitive and intransitive	X	X	X
Verbs with prepositions	X	X	X
Special finite verbs	X	X	X
Mood		X	X
Infinitives	X	X	X
Functions of the infinitive		X	X
Participles		X	X
The functions of the participles			X

Nouns (Pages 60-64)

in the 5th grade, the following concepts of nouns were taught: plurals, collective nouns, and possessive nouns. Repeat them each year. The most important topic for the sixth grade is the possessive case. This is complicated. Give them many examples to work with.

Learning the gerunds is best in the seventh or eighth grades.

Nouns	5th	6th	7th	8th
Plurals	X	X	X	X
Collective nouns	X	X	X	X
Possessive nouns	X	X	X	X
Possessive case		X	X	X
Grammatical functions			X	X
Gerunds			X	X

The Teacher's Manual for Three Workbooks

Adjectives (Pages 65-75)

Adjectives	5th	6th	7th	8th
Positive, comparative, superlative	x	X	x	X
Position of adjectives		x	x	
The order of adjectives Grammar Rule 39, page 85	x	x	x	
Ordering adjectives continued Punctuation Rule 7, on page 120		X	x	X
Used attributively		X	x	X
Used predicatively		X	x	X
Adjectives as nouns		X	x	X
Nouns as adjectives			x	X
Participles as adjectives			x	X
Forming the negative with adjectives		X	x	X
Possessive adjectives		X	x	X
Interrogative adjectives		X	x	X

Adjectives are a simple and fun way to begin the school year before you cover more demanding categories of grammar. Develop their vocabulary as much as possible. How can you help children find new adjectives to use in their writing and speaking? The order of adjectives was introduced in the *English Workbook for Fifth Grade* on page 85 as Grammar Rule 39. This is important to repeat at the start of the sixth grade.

Then repeat it once more, when you work on the chapters on adjectives in the sixth to eighth grades. I would repeat the order of adjectives again, when you work on the chapter on *Punctuation* where you find the concepts described, in more detail, on page 120 as Punctuation Rule 7.

Adverbs (Pages 76-83)

Adverbs are also easy to learn at the beginning of the school year. How they act in the sentences is more complicated than many children realize. Spend time using adverbs to modify the verbs, the adjectives, and other adverbs. Build on their vocabulary as much as possible. How can you help chhildren find new adverbs to use in their writing and speaking? The challenge is also to find ways for them to use the adverbs they learn.

Adverbs	5th	6th	7th	8th
Positive, comparative, superlative	X	X	X	X
Where, when, and why	X			
Well and good	X	X	X	X
Types of adverbs		X	X	X
Adverbs and adjectives		X	X	X

Pronouns (Pages 84-103)

Pronouns always demand repetition. There are not many new topics in the sixth grade.

Pronouns	4th	5th	6th	7th	8th
Conjugation	X	X	X		
Reflexive pronouns	X	X	X	X	X
Interrogative pronouns	X	X	X	X	X
Nominative & objective case		X	X	X	X
Relative pronouns		X	X	X	X
Possessive pronouns			X	X	X
So and one			X	X	X
Demonstrative			X	X	X
Indefinite				X	X
Distributive				X	X

Prepositions (Pages 107-115)

For children to become accurate with their use of prepostions they need to practice choosing among the alternatives. Is the table on, above, behind, beside or under the floor? Notice how such a question raises pictures in your consciousness. This is fun and creative.

Prepositions	4th	5th	6th	7th	8th
Prepositions of place	X	X	X	X	X
Prepositions of time	X	X	X	X	X
Prepositional phrases		X	X	X	X
Prepositions and adverbs			X	X	X
Phrasal verbs			X	X	X

The Teacher's Manual for Three Workbooks

Conjunctions (Pages 116-118)

This is a very important topic in the sixth grade. What is the difference between coordinating and subordinating parts of a sentence and the use of conjunctions? These are the two main concepts you need to develop. Then practice using them.

Conjunctions	6th	7th	8th
Coordinating conjunctions	X	x	X
Subordinating conjunctions	X	x	X
Correlative conjunctions		x	X

Punctuation (Pages 119-126)

Your work with punctuation becomes much more demanding in the sixth grade. Now you can review and further develop direct speech and dialogues. Take your time on this part of the curriculum. The children need a lot of practice to become accurate.

They should also learn to use colons, dashes, hyphens, parentheses, slashes, and ellipses.

You can develop punctuation while working on the other chapters of the workbook. When you work regularly throughout the year, the children's accuracy will improve.

Punctuation	4th	5th	6th	7th	8th
Periods	X	x	X		
Question and exclamation marks	X	x	X		
Capitalization	X	x	X	x	X
Dialogue/direct speech		x	X	x	X
Colon		x	X	x	X
Semicolon		x	X	x	X
Commas	X	x	X	x	X
Titles		x	X	x	X
Placement of adjectives			X	x	X
Dashes, hyphen			X	x	X
Ellipses, slashes, parenthesis			X	x	X
Italics			X	x	X

Irregular Verb List (Pages 146-151)

Do your pupils need more work with the irregular verbs? Is their spelling accurate? I found it helpful to continue with regular, weekly dictations of sentences using irregular verbs. Ask them to memorize five irregular verbs in three tenses. Memorization is very important and it needs to be practiced regularly. Children with writing challenges especially need regular practice.

Fragmented sentences & Improper shifts

You may include improper shifts in the more simple categories of person, number, and use of pronouns. Build this into your work with nouns, verbs, and pronouns.

Fragmented sentences & Improper shifts	6th	7th	8th
Shifts in person	X	x	X
Shifts in number	x	x	X
Shifts in pronouns	x	x	X

Suggestions for the seventh grade

Now your pupils are twelve and going on thirteen. Grammar is a great subject for them to learn. Whatever you introduced last year should be repeated this year at a new level, giving all of the children a new chance to gain confidence in their skills. Use a good sense of humor and appeal to their intellect in a new way. Give them a good feeling in your lessons!

Make your own sentences to demonstrate the grammar through conversation. Then let them develop their own examples. Forget the examples you have used and concentrate on the rules. Forget the rules and concentrate on how the language works. Then the children have the syntax and grammar at their fingertips to use.

Repeat what you have learned. Repeat, repeat, repeat is the mantrum of teaching grammar! This is crucial to concept development for your pupils each year. Use new sides of your sense of humor. Make grammar fun to learn at a new level and with new methods.

Types of sentences and word positioning (Pages 8-11)

In the sixth grade, the pupils learned to distinguish between simple and compound sentences. Now they learn how clauses form complex sentences and compound-complex sentences. A simple way to approach compound-complex sentences is to first make a compound sentence. Then add a clause to one of the sentences or to both of the sentences in the compound sentence.

Word positioning helps the children discover how the words are used and where they are used in the sentence.

Types of sentences and word positioning	6th	7th	8th
Simple sentences	x	x	x
Compound sentences	x	x	x
Complex sentences		x	x
Compound-complex sentences		x	x
The position of nouns		x	x
The position of adjectives		x	x

Parts of speech (Pages 14-16)

There are nine parts of speech that the pupils may identify in a sentence. Depending on the level of understanding in the class, I start the year with such exercises, or I wait for several months. Sometimes I work on parts of speech twice during the school year.

Sentence analysis (page 17)

Develop simple sentences with the subject-predicate combination and add the object, then the indirect object. Give the students examples to work with and let them write their own sentences for analysis. Your students may enjoy working in groups as they develop sentences for each other and then correct each other.

Sentence analysis	6th	7th	8th
Subject & predicate	X	x	x
Complete predicate	X	x	x
Subject, predicate, object		x	x
Subject, predicate, object, indirect object		x	x
Kinds of clauses found in Clauses 2			x
Function of the clauses			x

Phrases (Page 18)

In the seventh grade, the pupils may differentiate between noun phrases, verb phrases, adjective phrases, adverb phrases, and prepositional phrases

Clauses 1 (Pages 19-37)

Major new concepts are on the agenda for this year: relative adverbs, adverb clauses, adjective clauses, noun clauses, and conditional clauses.

Clauses 1	6th	7th	8th
Independent clauses	X	X	x
Dependent clauses	X	X	x
Complex sentences	X	X	x
Relative pronouns introduce relative clauses	X	X	x
Relative adverbs introduce relative clauses		X	x
Adjective clauses		X	x
Noun clauses		X	x
Adverb clauses		X	x
Conditional clauses		X	x

Verbs (Pages 46-59)

Participles play an important role in the English language. When teenagers learn to use them, their thinking becomes more flexible. Participles are forms of the verbs in different tenses; for instance, walking, walked, and walk are all participles of the verb to walk. These forms of the verbs may be used as adjectives as, "The *walked* dog is happy."

Other participles may be used as nouns; for instance, " *Walking* is important for your dog." A participle used as a noun is called a gerund.

I would begin with partiples in the seventh grade. Take your time in allowing the pupils to discover for themselves which forms of the verbs are used as adjectives and which as gerunds. The gerunds are on pages (60 -82). Start with simple participles that your pupils already use without calling them participles; for example, "The *written* statement is accurate." You may want to spend two or three lessons using participles without giving them a name. The next step is to ask the pupils where the verb tense form, *written* comes from? They have used it as an adjective but it is originally a verb. Challenge them to find out on their own. Give many more examples. The next step may be to look at the verb matrix. Ask them to fill out the verb matrix with the verb, to *write*. Is the adjective *written* to be found in the matrix? Do this with many more examples: crooked, broken, forgotten, or flown, to name a few.

Now you may look at the difference between regular and iregluar verbs. Ask them to read the irregular verb list on pages (146 - 151) to see if they can find the forms of verbs that may become adjectives in a sentence. Make an exercise where they must write ten senteces with verb forms as adjectives.

Finally, you give them the name *participles* as a concept in a meaningful relation with their concept of verbs and adjectives.

The Teacher's Manual for Three Workbooks

One month later, you may refresh their memory by asking the abstract question, "What is a participle?" Do the same with the concept of the gerund.

Nouns (Pages 60-64)

Repeat the possessive case with singular and plural nouns. Then teach or review gerunds. This work may be related to the progressive tense, for you use the participle from the progressive tense as a noun (a gerund) or as gerund phrase. For gerunds see pages 60 and 61 in the workbook.

Nouns	5th	6th	7th	8th
Plurals	x	x	x	x
Collective nouns	x	x	x	x
Possessive nouns	x	x	x	x
Possessive case		x	x	x
Grammatical functions		x	x	x
Gerunds			x	x

Adjectives (Pages 65-75)

The only new concepts are nouns as adjectives and participles as adjectives. See the verb section above for the concept of using a verb form, the participle, as an adjective. The irregular verb list will be helpful for the pupils to discover new participles.

Adjectives	5th	6th	7th	8th
Positive, comparative, superlative	x	x	x	x
Position of adjectives	x	x		
The order of adjectives Grammar Rule 39, page 85	x			
Ordering adjectives continued Punctuation Rule 7, on page 120		x	x	x
Used attributively		x	x	x
Used predicatively		x	x	x
Adjectives as nouns		x	x	x
Nouns as adjectives			x	x
Participles as adjectives			x	x
Forming the negative with adjectives		x	x	x
Possessive adjectives		x	x	x
Interrogative adjectives		x	x	x

Adverbs (Pages 76-83)

Repeat the concepts they have developed with adverbs and build their vocabulary of adverbs. Can you discover fun ways to teach them to use adverbs more frequently and accurately in writing and in speech?

Pronouns (Pages 84-103)

The new categories are indefinite pronouns and distributive pronouns. You will also need to focus on relative pronouns and how they introduce clauses.

Pronouns	4th	5th	6th	7th	8th
Conjugation	X	x	x		
Reflexive pronouns	X	x	x	X	X
Interrogative pronouns	X	x	x	X	X
Nominative & objective case		x	x	X	X
Relative pronouns		x	x	X	X
Possessive pronouns			x	X	X
So and one			x	X	X
Demonstrative			x	X	X
Indefinite				X	X
Distributive				X	X

Antecedents (Pages 104-106)

Antecedents are a new concept for the children. You may introduce them as words, phrases, or clauses. The antecedent is a word, phrase, or clause to which a following pronoun refers to. *The boy could not remember where he parked the car.* He refers to the boy. Boy is the antecedent of he.

See pages 104-106 for more examples.

Antecedents	6th	7th	8th
Antecedents as a word		x	x
Antecedents as a phrase		x	x
Antecedents as a clause		x	x

The Teacher's Manual for Three Workbooks

Prepositions (Pages 107-115)

All you need to do is move through the chapter one more time and create your own exercises based on the pupils' experiences.

Conjunctions (Pages 116-118)

Correlative conjunctions are the new category you should introduce. The correlative conjunctions connect parts of the sentence that have mutual relationships in which one clause depends on the other clause. They may correlate words or phrases as well.

Later, you can compare them with coordinating and subordinating conjunctions. The coordinating conjunctions match two clauses that make parallel statements.

The subordinating conjunctions connect clauses that provide further information to the main sentence.

Conjunctions	6th	7th	8th
Coordinating conjunctions	X	x	X
Subordinating conjunctions	X	x	X
Correlative conjunctions		x	X

Punctuation (Pages 119 -126)

Relate the chapter to the pupils' experiences by rewriting and asking them to identify where they are unsure of proper use.

Fragmented sentences & Improper shifts (Pages 127 -146)

In the seventh grade, I suggest you cover all of the improper shifts.

Fragmented sentences & Improper shifts	6th	7th	8th
Shifts in person	x	x	X
Shifts in number	x	x	X
Shifts in pronouns	x	x	X
Shifts in tenses		x	X
Shifts in voice		x	X

Suggestions for the eighth grade

Fourteen-year-olds will have learned plenty of grammar. Now they can use their knowledge of grammar to improve their writing style, their reading comprehension, and their speech. Work with more complicated texts about nature, science, economics, politics, and all other subjects that interest your pupils.

The work this year will be more rigorous. Start again by reviewing the seventh grade grammar within two or three weeks.

Types of sentences & word positioning (pages 8 – 13)

Review this at a more complicated level of learning. You thereby challenge them to stretch their understanding.

Parts of Speech (pages 14 – 16)

Review at new level of learning which your pupils need. Use more complicated sentences as you move forward.

Sentence analysis (page 17)

There is only one page in the workbook about sentence analysis, but there are two chapters on clauses, which are a major part of it. Once you have covered both chapters on clauses you may begin to analyze what the clause does in the sentence.

The function of the clause is to modify the verb, qualify the noun, make a statement, or act as the object:

> The girl said *that she was hungry.*

That she was hungry is the object of said. It is a noun clause.

> *The boy who was swimming saw a turtle.*

Who was swimming qualifies the boy and is an adjective clause.

> *He laughed as if his stomach would burst.*

As if his stomach would burst modifies laughed and is an adverb clause.

The Teacher's Manual for Three Workbooks

He spoke as if it was not his problem.

As if it was not his problem modifies he spoke and is a conditional clause.

Sentence analysis	6th	7th	8th
Subject & predicate	x	X	x
Complete predicate	x	X	x
Subject, predicate, object		X	x
Subject, predicate, object, direct object		X	x
Kinds of clauses found in Clauses 2			x
Function of the clauses			x

Phrases (page 18)

Review from the seventh grade concept development on page 51 of this manual.

Clauses 1 (pages 19 – 37)

Review the chapter on clauses 1, then work on clauses 2.

Clauses 1	6th	7th	8th
Independent clauses	x	x	x
Dependent clauses	x	x	x
Complex sentences	x	x	x
Relative pronouns introduce relative clauses	x	x	x
Relative adverbs introduce relative clauses		x	x
Adjective clauses		x	x
Noun clauses		x	x
Adverb clauses		x	x
Conditional clauses		x	x

Clauses 2 (pages 38 – 45)

Clauses 2	6th	7th	8th
Restrictive & non-restrictive clauses			x
Analysis of clauses			x
Clauses in complicated text			x

Restrictive and Non-restrictive Clauses

In the 5th grade, this subject was simply introduced. It was established that parenthetical elements are groups of words that add or clarify the meaning of a sentence.

This is rather complicated for your pupils, so you need to begin slowly.

What is a parenthetical element? A parenthetical element is a word, or group of words such as a phrase, or clause that add to or clarify the meaning of the sentence. Lead the class to the understanding of this concept.

> The beach, which is white, is covered with sand dollars freshly deposited by the surf.
>
> The store that closed was my favorite.

Next develop the concept of what a restrictive and non-restrictive parenthetical element is. Parenthetical elements are named restrictive and non-restrictive according to their use in the sentence.

Restrictive elements are needed to understand the sentence's meaning.

> The dog that saved his owner from the fire was brave.

Here we know what the dog did in order to be called 'brave'.

Non-restrictive elements are not necessary to understand the meaning of the sentence. The non-restrictive elements are always enclosed in commas.

> The tree, which is old, lost many limbs in the storm.

The information that it is old, is not necessary to know that it has lost many limbs.

Whether the relative pronouns, *which* and *that* are used, indicates the difference between restrictive or non-restrictive parenthetical elements. *Which* is used with non-restrictive elements and *that* is used with restrictive elements. Commas are used with non-restrictive elements. Because of these rules, it is often easier to identify one, than it is to figure out how to write one yourself. The most important thing is to ask yourself if the parenthetical element is essential to the meaning of the sentence or not. Make sure the sentence says what you want it to say.

> The dress that I wore to the assembly needs to be cleaned. (restrictive)
>
> My dress, which is red, was torn yesterday. (non-restrictive)

In the 6th, 7th, and 8th grades, the awareness of how we use these parenthetical elements is expanded. Non-restrictive parenthetical elements can occur as words, phrases, or clauses.

> Gee, that is tough! (Here it is an interjection.)

Willis, from Canada, is an excellent hockey player. (Here it is a phrase.)

My lawn, which has grown quickly, needs to be cut. (Here it is a clause.)

Restrictive parenthetical elements can be found as a phrase (adjective), a clause (adjective), and an appositive.

The leaves from the old tree fell around my feet. (an adjective phrase)

The dappled grey horse that I know came to my side of the pasture.

(an adjective clause)

That man Woodson is a great conversationalist. (an appositive)

The relative pronouns *who, which, whose,* and *that* are used in these types of sentences. We have discussed *which* and *that* and their use with restrictive and non-restrictive parenthetical elements. *Who* can be used with either a restrictive or a nonrestrictive element.

The goalie on our team who is Canadian blocked the puck with his stick.

Here the word *goalie* is restricted: we know he is from Canada.

Compare that sentence with a new sentence containing the same subject, *goalie,* that is non-restrictive.

The goalie on our team, who drives a convertible, saved thirteen goals today.

The non-restrictive clause, *who drives a convertible* tells us that he likes cars. It does not matter that he likes cars. Nor does it matter that his car is a convertible. What matters is that he makes saves!

The relative pronoun *whose* can be used interchangeably as well.

That tabby cat whose owner I know well disappeared last night.

The young author, whose name I forgot, is speaking tonight.

Use *which* restrictively only with a preposition.

The bucket in which I poured the milk had a small leak in its side.

Verbs (pages 46 – 59)

The verb tenses and the matrix are very important in the eighth grade. Make sure to practice them well.

Verbs	6th	7th	8th
The verb matrix	X	X	X
Active and passive voice	X	X	X
Transitive and intransitive	X	X	X
Verbs with prepositions	X	X	X
Special finite verbs	X	X	X
Mood		X	X
Infinitives	X	X	X
Functions of the infinitive		X	X
Participles		X	X
The functions of the participles			X

Review direct and indirect speech, active and passive voice, the special finite verbs, and moods.

There are twelve special finite verbs that help other verbs form the interrogative, negative, and emphatic forms of speech. They also form tenses, mood, and voice.

The mood of the verb shows what a verb is doing and the manner in which the action is taking place. It also shows how the speaker thinks.

There are three main moods. The imperative mood is a command, suggestion, or invitation. The subjunctive mood expresses a wish. The indicative mood makes statements or asks questions. This is the most common mood.

Review verbs used as participles. Remind your pupils of simple rules such as the following: The present participle of regular verbs uses -ing. The past participle of regular verbs uses –ed.

Remind them that many present and past participles can be used as adjectives. The adjective participles may be modified by adverbs such as *very, too,* or *quite.* They can make a mood of comparison by adding more or most. Look at your list of irregular verbs for participles that can be used as adjectives.

Then show your pupils how participles appear as adjective clause equivalents and as adverb clause equivalents. Here is a participle used as an adverb clause equivalent. *Talking as fast as he could*, the boy was trembling.

For more examples see page 58.

Participles may also appear as participial phrases, "*Looking out the window*, I saw an eagle."

They may also be used with the infinitive of the verb, "*To be* or *not to be, that is the question!"*

For further information on the particples see the gerund section on pages () where the difference between using particples as gerunds or as adjectives if explained.

Nouns (pages 60 - 64)

Review the content on nouns in the *English Workbook for Fifth Grade* and review the content in this workbook on pages 60 to 64.

Gerunds

A gerund acts like a noun, and is made from a verb; for example, "Swimming is fun." *Swimming* is the gerund, acting like a noun. Gerunds have the same form as a participle (swimming).

If used as a phrase, they can have a subject and an object. The subject is usually in the possessive case.

>His *knowing* the right answer made the bet unfair.

Now you can help your pupils discover for themselves which forms of the verbs are used as adjectives and which as gerunds. They have used gerunds all their lives, but now we are teaching them to become conscious of it. The gerunds are on pages 60 -62.

Remember that all of the forms of verbs in every tense are participles. Not all of the forms may be used as adjectives. Not all of the forms may be used as nouns we call gerunds.

Start with simple participles your pupils already use without calling them participles; for instance the sentence, *The written statement is accurate.*

You may spend two or three lessons using participles without giving them a name. This gives the pupils practice. The next step is to ask the pupils where the verb tense form, *written* comes from? They have used it as an adjective, but it was originally a verb. Challenge them to find out which tense the participle comes from on their own. Give many more examples.

The next step may be to look at the verb matrix. Ask them to fill out the verb matrix with the verb, to write. Is the adjective *written* to be found in the matrix? Do this with many more examples: crooked, broken, forgotten, or flown to name a few.

You will need to practice gerunds and participles in order to be comfortable with them. Now you may look at the irregluar verbs that may be used as adjectives. Ask them to read the irregular verb list on pages 146 – 151 to see if they find the forms of verbs that may be used as adjectives in a sentence. Some of the irregular verb, perfect tense participles work, and some of them do not work as adjectives in a sentence. A few of the irregular, past tense particples work as adjectives, if the same word is used in the past tense as in the perfect tense.

Remember that the rules are different with the regular verb participles because all you do is add 'ed'. Omit 'to'. The *walked dog is happy. Walked* is a regular verb participle in the past and the perfect tense.

Make an exercise where they must write ten senteces with verb forms as adjectives.

Finally you give them the names *participles* and *gerunds* as a concept in a meaningful relation with their concept of verbs, adjectives, and nouns.

Appositives

Appositives are nouns, noun phrases, or noun clauses that rename or describe another noun used in the sentence. We use commas, brackets, or dashes to emphasize the appositive.

> 44 Downing Street, *my address,* is well known in Wilkes-Barre.
>
> *My sister*, Jean, just did a backflip.
>
> The book (The Last Train) is easy to read.
>
> The friendly dog, namely a German shepherd, crossed the road towards me.
>
> Thomas Jefferson, *who wrote a significant part of the Declaration of Independence,* owned Montebello in Virginia. (comma)
>
> Thomas Jefferson (*who wrote a significant part of the Declaration of Independence*) owned Montebello in Virginia. (bracket)
>
> Thomas Jefferson - *who wrote a significant part of the Declaration of Independence* - owned Montebello in Virginia. (dash)

Adjectives (pages 65 - 75)

Repeat everything from the seventh grade content.

Adverbs (pages 76 – 83)

Adverbs that tell *how, when,* and *where*, not only modify verbs, other adverbs, and

The Teacher's Manual for Three Workbooks

adjectives but they occasionally modify a noun.

The interrogative adverbs are *why and how.*

How did you find us?

Why did you ask that?

Adverbs of affirmation

Yes	Yes, I know him.
Certainly	I certainly will.
Surely	Surely you understand.

Adverbs of probability

| Perhaps | Perhaps we will attend the party. |
| Maybe | Maybe I can join you. |

Adverbs of negation

No	No, I do not know him.
Not	We will not attend the party.
Never	I will never join you.

Adverbs of quantity, amount, or number:

Little	You only need a little salt.
Twice	She called twice.
Once	Once I decide, I am active.

Relative adverbs make a relative clause:

| When | I remember when you came to our party. |
| Where | This is the room where Lincoln slept in Gettysburg. |

Discuss the differences between the types of adverbs: affirmation, probability, negation, quantity, amount, and number. These are key concepts for the teenager to learn.

Chapters with no new key concepts

Review the following chapters though there are no new key concepts to present. You allow the pupils to redevelop the concepts they already have from the seventh grade.

Pronouns (pages 84 – 103) **Antecedents (pages 104 – 106)**

Prepositions (pages 107 – 115) **Conjunctions (pages 116 – 118)**

Punctuation (Pages 119 – 126)

Fragmented Sentences and Improper Shifts (page 127 – 145)

The fragmented sentences are a good topic in the eighth grade. It will help them improve their writing styles and later they will recognize this in the SATs.

Fragmneted sentences & Improper shifts	6th	7th	8th
Shifts in person	X	X	x
Shifts in number	X	X	x
Shifts in pronouns	X	X	x
Shifts in tenses		X	x
Shifts in voice		X	x
Shifts in mood			x
Improper shifts in mood			x
Inappropriate shifts in speech			x
Inappropriate shifts in tone			x
Parallel srtructure in words & phrases			x
Mixed constructions			x
Fragmented sentences			x
Illogical coordination			x
Dangling modifiers			x

Irregular Verb List (pages 146 – 151)

Use the list to find participles made from irregular verbs.

Preparing for Tests (page 152 - 154)

When I prepare my students for a test or exam, I tell them a few weeks in advance exactly what they need to learn to do well. Here the workbook comes in handy. I name the sections to learn for the grammar part. They can also look at the Index at the end of the workbook.

I. **Grammar from the Workbbok you need to know**

1. Verb matrix   Page 4
2. Parts of speech   p. 12 - 14
3. Phrases   p. 16
4. Clauses: p. 17 – 37
5. Verbs   p. 47 - 57
6. Adjectives: p. 65 - 74
7. Adverbs: p. 75 - 83
8. Pronouns   p. 84 - 108
9. Prepositions: p. 109 – 113
10. Nouns   p. 61 – 66
11. Gerunds   p. 61
12. Participles   p. 70- 71

Then I give them questions to practice.

I. **Random questions for preparation**

1. What is a phrase?
2. Write a sentence with a noun clause.

3. What is a paragraph?
4. Write a sentence with an adjective clause.
5. Write a paragraph in the past progressive tense.
6. Write a sentence with an adjective phrase.
7. Write a paragraph in the future perfect tense.
8. Write a sentence with a conditional clause.
9. Write the verb matrix.
10. What is a clause?
11. Use five words as gerunds in sentences.
12. Use five irregular verbs as participles in sentences.
13. Find six nouns in your dictionary, find their plural form, and use them in sentences in the possessive form.

We practice answering the questions in class, first individually, then in groups to help each other find the answers.

Index (pages 155 – 157)

Ask them to look up topics using the index as a reference. Give them problems to solve and let them find their own answers.

Suggestions for yearly planning

Below is an overview of chapters in the workbook with my suggestions for what to cover year by year.

Overview

	6th	**7th**	**8th**
Repeat content from previous year	X	x	X
Types of sentences & word positioning	X	x	X
Parts of speech	X	x	X
Sentence analysis			x
Phrases		x	x
Clauses 1		x	x
Clauses 2			x
Verbs	X	x	x
Nouns	X	x	x
Adjectives	X	x	x
Adverbs	X	x	x
Pronouns	X	x	x
Antecedents			x
Prepositions	X	x	x
Conjunctions	X	x	x
Punctuation	X	x	x
Fragmented sentences	x	x	x
Improper shifts	X	x	x
Irregular verb list	X	x	x
Preparing for tests		x	x
Index			x

And below you may mark your own topics to cover each year.

Your plan

	6th	**7th**	**8th**
Repeat content from previous year			
Types of sentences & word positioning			
Parts of speech			
Sentence analysis			
Phrases			
Clauses 1			
Clauses 2			
Verbs			
Nouns			
Adjectives			
Adverbs			
Pronouns			
Antecedents			
Prepositions			
Conjunctions			
Punctuation			
Fragmented sentences			
Improper shifts			
Irregular verb list			
Preparing for tests			
Index			

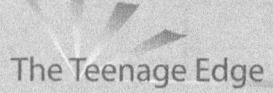

List of Content in the Sixth to Eighth Grade Workbook

Adjectives 14
    Coordinate 120
    Cumulative 120
    Demonstrative 89
    Forming the negative 71
    Interrogative 74
    Order of 120
    Position of, 12
    Possessive 73,86
    Used as nouns 67
    Used attributively 12,65
    Used predicatively 66

Adverbs 14,76
    Adverbial phrases 83
    Comparison of 79
    Game 83
    Of affirmation 76
    Of frequency 12,82
    Interrogative 76
    Modify adjectives 80
    Modify verbs 8
    Of manner 12,82
    Of negation 76
    Of place 12,82
    Of probability 76
    Of quality 76
    Of time 12,82
    Position of 12
    With prefexes 78
    With suffixes 78

Adverbial phrases 13,18

Antecedent 104-106
    As a word 104
    As a phrase 104
    As a clause 104

Appositives 31

Articles 14

Charles Dickens
    Oliver Twist 44-45
    Great Expectations 124

Clauses
    Adjective clauses 21,29,30,39,43
    Adverb clauses 21,34,42
    Analysis of 42
    Conditional clauses 23,37,43
    Dependent clauses 9,10,11,21,22,42
    Independent clauses 9,10,11,19
    Main clauses 9, 21
    Non-defining, adjective clauses 39
    Noun clauses 21,31,32,42
    Relative clauses 26,30
    Restrictive and non-restrictive clauses 38-42

Complement 11,31,53

Complex sentences 9, 22

Compound sentences 8,9

Conjunctions 8,14
    Coordinating 8,9,116
    Correlative 118
    Subordinating 9,117

Constitution of the United States 124-126

Direct and indirect speech 119

English
    American 7,39,119,122
    British 7,39

Fragmentations 127-145
- Dangling modifiers 143
- Illogical coordination 143
- Mixed constructions 140
- Sentences 142

Improper Shifts 127
- In mood 130
- In number 127
- In person 127
- In pronouns 128
- In speech 136
- In tenses 129
- In tone 138
- In voice 135

Indirect object 60

Indirect speech 136-137

Interjections 14

Mood 49
- Conditional 49
- Imperative 49,132
- Improper shifts 132-134
- Indicative 49,132
- Interrogative 49
- Subjunctive 49,130

Nouns 14
- Appositives 63
- Grammatical function of 60
- Gerund 60
- Position of 11
- Possessive form 62,
- Used as adjectives 68

Object 17
- Direct 11,17, 60
- Indirect 11,60
- Of the preposition 11,60
- Of the verb 31,53,60

Paragraph 10,123

Parallel structure 139

Participles 55-59
- As adjective clause equivalent 58
- As adverb clause equivalent 58
- Compound 56
- Past with regular verbs 55
- Perfect made with irregular verbs 146-151
- Perfect active 55
- Perfect passive 56,57
- Position of 58
- Present passive 56
- Progressive 55
- Used as adjectives 57,70
- With infinitive 57

Parts of speech 14

Phrases 18-19
- Adjective phrases 18
- Adverbial phrases 18,83
- Gerund phrases 61
- Noun phrases 18
- Parallel structure 139
- Prepositional phrases 18, 141
- Verb phrases 18

Predicate 17

Predicate adjectives 31

Prefixes 71

Prepositions 14, 107
- And adverbs 113
- Game 108-109
- Group 108
- Of place 108
- Of time 111

Pronouns 14
- Both 93
- Demonstrative 89
- Distributive 97
- Improper shifts 128
- Indefinite 91
- Intensive 84
- Interrogative 100
- Other, another 94
- Possessive 86
- Reflexive 84
- Relative 9, 20, 26-29,
- So, one 87-88

Punctuation
- Colon 119

The Teacher's Manual for Three Workbooks

Comma, uses of, 8,9,73,121,123
Dash 121,122
Ellipses 122
Exclamation marks 121,123
Hyphen 121
Parentheses 122
Question mark 121,123
Quotation marks 121, 122,123
Semi-colon 119
Slash 122

Sentences,
    Affirmative 93
    Analysis of 17
    Complex 9
    Compound 9
    Compound-complex 10
    Interrogative 94
    Negative 94
    Simple 9
    Structure 8

Subject 11, 17

Subject – predicate combination 18,19

Suffixes 68

Tense of Verbs
    Future simple 6
    Future Progressive 6
    Future Perfect 6
    Future Perfect Progressive 6
    Past Progressive 6
    Past Perfect 6
    Past Perfect Progressive 6
    Past Simple 6
    Present Progressive 6
    Present Perfect 6
    Present Perfect Progessive 6
    Present Simple 6
    Shits 129

Tests 152-154

Verbs 14
    Irregular verb list 146-151
    Infinitive 52, 53
    Regular 55
    Phrasal 115
    Shall 7
    Special finite 48,52
    Transitive and intransitive 46
    Voice 135
    Will 7
    With prepositions 47

Word position 8

Suggestions for the Ninth Grade

The Teenage Edge

At the beginning of the year, repeat the development of concepts in all parts of speech. Wherever you discover categories of grammar the pupils are still unsure of, go into the details of that category one more time.

You may develop another series of exercises by asking them to look up a category in the workbook and make new examples. For instance, ask your pupils to look up participial phrases and have them write sentences with two of them.

When your pupils have learned the grammar in this workbook they have developed a lot of logical thinking. Now the pupils can use their knowledge of grammar to work with the Categories of Aristotle. The Categories of Aristotle include many grammatical ideas and they help the pupil dive deeper and deeper into any subject they choose from many perspectives. The being or substance you choose to learn about is viewed from ten perspectives. You may choose a person, a plant, an animal, or a star. Everything is possible. When pupils write reports or a thesis, the categories will help them develop their knowledge. They can reach a deeper understanding of their topic. With each category there is a question to be asked and answered.

1. Substance or Being — Who or what?
2. Quantity — What is necessary for the being or substance?
3. Quality — What is the quality?
4. Relation — To what is the being related ?
5. Place — Where is the being or substance placed?
6. Time — When does the being or substance evolve?
7. Position — Where does the being or substance grow?
8. State — How will it develop?
9. Action — What do I do?
10. Undergoing something — How am I affected?

Aristotle challenges his pupils to learn more about what they are studying. Once the pupil has examined the porcupine he has decided to write about, he can choose two or three or four categories; place, time, state, and action for example. This will open new questions concerning the porcupines life. Another pupil may be writing about his hero and start comparing categories like action and time, or quality and place. The possibilities are unlimited. The questions open the door to gaining new knowledge.

"None of these terms is used on its own in any statement, but it is through their combination with one another that a statement comes into being. For every statement is held to be either true or false." Aristotle

Sources

Oxford Advanced Learner´s Dictionary of Current English, Oxford University Press, A S Hornby, Fifth Edition, Editor Jonathan Crowther, 1995

C.E. Eckersley qnd J. M. Eckersley, *The Comprehensive English Grammar For Foreign Students,* Longman, 1960.

Heinz Zimmermann, *Grammatikk, Spiel von Bewegung und Form*, Verlag am Goetheanum, 1997.

J. Smit, articles *Picture and Concept, The Past, Present and Future, Subject, Predicate and Object in Grammar,* and *A Little Introduction To Grammar*, in The Waldorf Journal Project #16, AWSNA, October 2010.

The Common Core State Standards, English Language Arts Standards, Grades 4-8, published by the National Governors Association Center for Best Practices, Council of Chief State School Officers, Washington DC in 2010.

A complete list of books by Ted Warren

Freedom as Spiritual Activity, Temple Lodge Publications, London, 1994

The Teenage Edge, Guiding Teens To Their Unique Strengths,

AWSNA, Boulder, 2005

English Workbook for Fourth Grade, 2014

English Workbook for Fifth Grade, 2015

English Workbook for Sixth to Eighth Grades, 2017

The Teacher`s Manual for Three Workbooks: Fourth Grade, Fifth Grade and Sixth Grade to Eighth Grade, 2017

ESL I, English as a Second Language for Beginners, 2015

ESL II, English as a Second Language for Intermediate Learners, 2015

ESL III, English as a Second Language for Almost Experts, 2017

The Teacher`s Manual for Three ESL Workbooks, 2017

Underway for 2019:

Revolutions in The Valley, Local, National and World History for Teenagers

**Please contact me or order books
on my website:**

Ted Warren

www.teenage-edge.org

email: ted.warren@teenage-edge.org